LIVING & LOVING

Mutually

Living and Loving Mutually: How To Break Free From Hurtful Relationship Patterns.

For information regarding licensing this content, or to order in bulk, write to Connection Victory Publishing Company at <inforequest@connectionvictory.com> or use the contact form on our website: www.ConnectionVictory.com/contact

Author: Avrum G. Weiss, Ph.D.
Editor: Wilhelm Cortez
Associate Editor: E.G. Regan
Photo of Author: Julia Curran Photography

ISBN: 978-1-64381-031-7 (paperback)
ISBN: 978-1-64381-032-4 (ePub)
ISBN: 978-1-64381-030-0 (PDF)
ISBN: 978-1-64381-033-1 (MOBI)
ASIN: B08JWTJDLF (Kindle)

Disclaimer: Although this publication is designed to provide accurate information with regard to the subject matter covered, the publisher and the author assume no responsibility for errors, inaccuracies, omissions, or any other inconsistencies herein. This publication is meant as a source of valuable information for the reader, however it is not meant as a replacement for direct expert assistance. If such level of assistance is required, the services of a competent professional should be sought.

LIVING & LOVING

Mutually

How To Break Free From Hurtful Relationship Patterns

Avrum G. Weiss, Ph.D.

Lasting
Impact
Press

Pontiac, Illinois

Advanced Praise for
Living and Loving Mutually

"In *Living and Loving Mutually*, Dr. Weiss offers simple, practical, and reassuring advice for some of the most common and pernicious issues that couples face in their relationships."

– Harris O'Malley, dating advice columnist,
Paging Dr. NerdLove
www.doctornerdlove.com

"Avrum Weiss is a gifted therapist who offers valuable insights and practices to bring couples closer together, providing realistic examples of the ways communication can foster understanding and overcome distance. In his book *Living and Loving Mutually*, his writing is clear, succinct, and goes straight to the heart of relationships, prompting a reader to agree, disagree, and laugh with recognition at the common issues that plague relationships. Avrum Weiss's relational perspective offers fresh ideas and practices to overcome these issues."

– Dana C. Jack, author of
Silencing the Self: Women and Depression
www.fairhaven.wwu.edu/users/djack

"Avrum Weiss's book *Living and Loving Mutually* is a good read. It provides a helpful collection of insightful ideas and actionable tools to help couples better understand themselves and each other so they can move forward in their relationship with confidence."

– Jacqui Olliver, Psychosexual Relationship Specialist
at End the Problem
www.endtheproblem.com/about

As a marriage, couples, and relationship therapist, I have often thought how nice it would be to offer men a playbook for navigating the surprisingly complex emotional currents in primary relationships. In *Living and Loving Mutually*, Dr. Avrum Weiss offers men an invaluable resource by addressing many of the common pitfalls that so often create pain, confusion, and distress within their love relationships. I appreciate Weiss's straightforward candor and clear, relatable examples of the predictable moments that send all of us into emotional quagmires with our partners. I highly recommend this book for any man wanting to show up more authentically and compassionately in their relationships.

Michael Barnett, LPC
Director of the Atlanta Center for
Emotionally Focused Therapy (EFT)
www.michaelbarnettlpc.com

Avrum G. Weiss, Ph.D.

Table of Contents

Dedication

For Michelle;
for helping me live a life
I never even dreamed of.

Introduction

"A baby alone doesn't exist." -- D.W. Winnicott

"There is no 'I' without a 'Thou'." -- Martin Buber

When we take that rare moment to pause and reflect, most of us realize that the most vital parts of our lives---the parts that bring us the most happiness and satisfaction---are the people we love and who love us. We are tribal creatures. We have achieved what we have as a species primarily due to our ability to sacrifice individual needs in the service of communal goals (Morris, 1999). Having strong and close relationships does more to keep you happy and healthy than even your genes do (Harvard, 2015). Conversely, the absence of close relationships is surprisingly harmful to both your physical and emotional health. Loneliness is as big a risk factor for cancer as smoking, and has been linked to premature mortality (Joiner, 2011).

Given the demonstrated importance of close relationships, it would seem that one of the most important things that the social sciences---particularly psychology---can do is to provide answers to the most pressing questions about how to find and maintain satisfying intimate relationships. Questions such as:

- *How do I know if this is the right person for me or am I just trying to talk myself into something so I won't be alone?*

- *How do I tell the difference between the kind of problems that every couple has and issues in my relationship that should concern me?*

- *What can we as a couple do to get through conflict in a healthy way that will help us feel closer and make our relationship stronger?*

- *If I've done everything I know how to do to make my relationship better and nothing seems to help, how do I know when it will be better for me to let go and move on?*

The Limitations of an Outdated Paradigm

If civilization is to survive, we must cultivate the science of human relationships: the ability of all peoples, of all kinds, to live together, in the same world at peace.

-- Franklin D. Roosevelt

The social sciences have contributed surprisingly few helpful answers to these important questions, largely because the assumptions of the natural sciences paradigm in which they operate constrict their research (Giorgi, 1988). We like to think that science reveals objective reality, helping to protect us from personal subjectivity and the political pressures that threaten to erode or even destroy those truths. However, all science operates within paradigms that shape not only what is studied within a given field, but also provides context that shapes how any field is understood.

My father told a joke about a cop walking his beat late at night and coming across a very drunk guy on his hands and knees, under a streetlamp, looking for something. The cop asked the guy what he was looking for, and the guy told him he was looking for his car keys. The cop asked if this was where he lost the keys and the guy told him, "no, but the lights much better here." The social sciences developed primarily under the streetlight of the natural sciences paradigm, not because their field of study was located there but because it was politically expedient to restrict the search to only what could be seen under the light (Giorgi, 1988). Many significant areas in the field---not the last of which have to do with relationships---are not well illuminated within the light of the natural sciences paradigm.

The primary limitation of the natural sciences paradigm for understanding relationships is an *a priori* assumption that individual needs are most important, and that relationships are a secondary means of attaining or interfering with individual needs. Psychological theories followed suit, conceptualizing individual development as a process of increasing separation and autonomy from the dependency of relationships (Erikson, 1968, Levinson, 1978). For example, Western cultures think of infants as helplessly dependent at birth and in need of training towards independence, but the Japanese see infants as independent at birth and in need of training towards mutual interdependency (Jordan, et al., 1991). Similarly, we think of the emotionally mature person as someone who is intimate with others by choice, but does not emotionally need anyone to be OK. Interestingly, in our culture, autonomy and independence are characterized as masculine qualities, while dependency is thought of as a feminine characteristic (Jordan, et al., 1991). Not surprisingly, we stereotypically attribute the desire for the inevitable mutual dependency of an intimate relationship to women, and portray men as resistant to interdependency as a threat to the satisfaction of their own individual needs (Weiss, 2002). In Western culture, we say *you can't love someone else until you love yourself.* We are less likely to recognize as equally true that loving and being loved by someone else are essential parts of coming to love oneself.

The Emergence of a New, Relational Paradigm

> *Everything is expressed through relationship. Colour can exist only through other colours, dimension through other dimensions, position through other positions that oppose them. That is why I regard relationships as the principal thing.*
>
> *– Piet Mondrian*

Paradigms are adopted when they successfully solve important problems or answer important questions, and they are modified or replaced when they no longer provide satisfactory answers (Kuhn, 1970). In psychology, a new relational paradigm has gradually emerged which offers potentially more satisfying explanations for important questions about relationships.

A relational approach starts with the assumption that relationships and the need for intimate connection with others are more important to us than the satisfaction of individual needs. There is an old Jewish parable about the difference between heaven and hell. In hell, everyone sits around a long table, loaded with all of the most sumptuous food imaginable, but they are all emaciated and starving because they each have an extremely long fork strapped to their forearms and can't manipulate the forks to bring food into their mouths. In heaven, the setup is exactly the same, but the people are well fed and happy because they reach across the table to feed each other. Reaching across the table to feed each other is the result of relational thinking.

From a relational perspective, it is only through intimate relationships that we become most fully ourselves. Each relationship elicits a different aspect of our potential in the same sense as the field of behavioral epigenetics discovered that different aspects of our genetic potential are either actuated or inhibited by environmental experiences (Moore, 2015). It's not just that we act and feel differently in the contexts of different relationships, it is that we literally are different people in each relationship. The self is actually created in the process of engaging in intimate relationships with others, or as philosopher Martin Buber (1937) most eloquently said: "There is no I without a thou." When a child is born, if someone picks that child up and gazes at them adoringly and holds them closely, that child understands herself as lovable in that moment and quite literally becomes lovable. She has no other frame of reference, she could not at that moment be anything else. If, however, that same child when born is cast aside in a trash bin, that child not only will experience herself as unlovable but will literally be unlovable. Again, she could not at that moment be anything else.

This understanding of the primacy of relationships is supported by substantial research on Attachment Theory, which demonstrated that early relationship experiences with caregivers rather than individual drives is what largely shapes our emotional and relationship development as adults, particularly in how we learn to manage emotional experience in relationships (Lyons-Ruth, et al., 2013). Recent developments in neuroscience also support a relational understanding of relationships. Neuroscientists have discovered that the brains of both humans and primates have a system of what are known as mirror neurons, which fire both when we act and when we observe the same action in another person. An everyday example is the way that people tend to unconsciously open their own mouths as they feed a baby. Scientists believe that mirror neurons are designed to help us empathically engage in relationships, and to live together in a social world (Preston, et al., 2002). Well known psychiatrist Dan Siegel (2010) suggests that mirror neurons are evidence that our brains are hardwired for connection.

From a relational perspective, reality is co-constituted by the people involved in the relationship. There is an Indian myth of the blind men and the elephant in which each man accurately describes the part of the elephant he is holding. The first man grabs the trunk and claims that what they are all holding is long, narrow and open at the end. Another man has a hold of a tusk and claims that what they are holding is hard and curved. Each man mistakenly believes that his experience alone is the whole truth. It is only when they share and honor each other's truths that they can understand that they are each holding a part of a larger truth that none of them alone can possibly understand.

In relationships, people accurately and often insistently describe their own experience, but then often make the error of insisting that whatever part they have a hold of represents the entirety of their mutually co-constituted reality. Relationships then become a power struggle, a zero-sum game in which one person's reality eventually prevails and the other person relinquishes her own truth and submits to the "truth" of the now dominant partner (Jack, 1993). As feminist psychologist Laura Brown said, "Objectivity is the name we give to the subjectivity of the dominant group." A relational approach equally honors the lived experience of all involved. In an old Sufi story, two people approach the judge. The first man states his case and the judge says "That's right." The second man states his case, completely contradicting everything that's just been said and the judge again agrees, "That's right." Exasperated, an observer exclaims, "Wait a minute, they completely disagreed. They can't both be right!" to which the judge replies, "That's right." A relational approach has the potential to minimize the blaming or pathologizing of either individual by equally honoring the experience of all involved.

Mutuality

The meeting of two personalities is like the contact of two chemical substances: if there is any reaction, both are transformed.

-- *Carl G. Jung*

The relationships that most enhance the potential for growth in each person are mutual relationships. In a mutual relationship, each person strives to be most fully and authentically him or herself. This requires a mutual capacity for empathy, with each person remaining aware of their own experience while also being interested in and empathic toward the experience of the other. Each person strives to participate fully in the relationship and is open to having an impact on and being impacted by the other, a mutual intersubjectivity (Jordan, et al., 1991).

A mutual relationship fosters the growth and development of both people. Said more strongly, "in order for a relation to be growth-enhancing for one person, it must be growth-enhancing for both people" (Jordan, et al., 1991). Conversely, any relationship that is damaging to one person is damaging to both. This has broad implications for our understanding of the harmful effects of the patriarchy on men as well as women.

When we fail in our efforts to understand each other---to be empathetic toward each other---then our relationships lack mutuality, which is the primary cause of pain and suffering in relationships. When we don't feel understood or cared about, the temptation is to distort ourselves in an effort to regain our mutual connection. As a result, we are most authentic when engaged in a mutually intimate relationships (Jordan, 2017).

The articles in this anthology are all written about relationships from a relational perspective. Part One is about issues in the early parts of a relationship. Part Two addresses communication in a developing relationship. Part Three explores how conflict develops in relationships and tips for resolving it. Part Four looks at sexual intimacy in relationships and Part Five takes up the issue of love.

Part One

Attraction

Attraction remains one of life's greatest mysteries. Despite the claims of many dating sites, we still don't really know much about what makes people attracted to each other. Many of you have probably spent significant time in a relationship that never really felt right but looked so good on paper, perhaps even criticizing yourself for being attracted to the wrong kind of person. If not, you certainly know couples who have been happily together for years or decades and you still can't figure out what makes them tick. If you are in a long-term relationship you almost certainly have moments when you look at your partner and wonder what in the world you are doing with someone who is so different from you. This first section will help you understand attraction from a more mutual perspective.

Chapter 1

A Shrink's Take on Dating

Hint: It's supposed to be fun.

I'm a clinical psychologist, and over the years, and I've had a lot of opportunities to work with people who are dating: either for the first time, or the first time in a long time. People generally describe dating as a miserable experience and approach it with emotions ranging from anxiety to terror. In fact, I've had a number of people tell me that they've stayed in bad marriages for years just because they dreaded dating so much.

A lot of dating advice seems to be taken from the "How to Be Popular in High School" manual. There are usually a lot of over-complicated tips for how to present a façade that will get people to like you. Following this advice, people obsess over writing the perfect profile for a dating website, or picking something to do for their first date that they think will really impress their date. In contrast, the most important thing I've learned about dating, and the thing that people most often overlook is very simple: just be yourself.

The purpose of dating is not to impress someone: it's not a job interview or a popularity contest. The objective is not to go out with as many people as you can or get as many people to like you as possible, it is to find one person you like, preferably someone who also likes you, and then spend some time together to see how things go.

Dating is about discernment. The idea is not to get someone to like you, but to figure out if you like each other. If you go out with someone on a first date and things don't click, that's a success, not a failure. Trying to impress someone to get them to like you creates the same problems as trying to impress an employer to get a job. If you succeed, then you have to continue to pretend to be someone you are not. In the long run, you are better served being yourself and letting the chips fall where they may.

Here are some of the most important things I've learned about dating:

Date a lot of people casually, and then one person at a time seriously. Don't spend a lot of time chatting online, texting, building up to a phone call, etc. None of that really helps you get to know someone, and it creates way too many opportunities for you to talk yourself out of meeting someone for purely imagined reasons. No matter how much the technology improves, there is still no substitute for good old-fashioned, face-to-face meeting. It's still the most reliable way to tell if you and another person will connect. If you have any interest in someone, don't waste a lot of time trying to figure things out. Go ahead and meet them for coffee and see what happens.

Don't obsess about when to text or call someone, whether it's too soon and you'll look needy, or how long you should wait, etc. Keep it simple. If you want to talk to someone, call them. If you don't, don't call them. Hopefully they will use the same straightforward principle with you, and then it's very easy to figure out where they stand. If they call you, you know they want to talk to you. If they don't call, you can be pretty sure they are not that interested in talking.

The criteria for going on a second date with someone is whether you had a good time on the first date. Again, keep it simple. If you enjoyed yourself see them again. Don't worry about whether they've been single long enough, or too long, or they're not into you enough or too into you, or too old or too young, or whatever other arcane criteria you've been using for dating. Keep it simple, if you had a good time, see them again. If you didn't have such a great time, but it was at least pleasant, and your intuition is that things might go better the next time, then go ahead and see them again. People are often very anxious on a first date and don't put their best foot forward. If you hope to be in a relationship with someone for the rest of your life, then what you are looking for is not how they are right now, but how they change and adapt over time. This is a long-term investment you are considering, so see them again and you may be pleasantly surprised.

Believe it or not, dating should be fun. Suggest things to do that are fun, things you like to do, not things you think the other person might like. If you suggest something fun that you like, the chances are better than you will be more relaxed and let more of your true self show through. Having coffee is fine for a first date, but it's a lot of unnecessary pressure to have date after date where all you do is sit and talk with each other.

Get out and do something fun, something silly where you get a chance to let your hair down and get to know each other in a variety of ways. Dating is a part of your social life, it's not a job. If dating starts to feel like a job, you probably should take a break and spend more time with your friends.

Think of dating as a great way to learn more about yourself. Every person you date gives you very helpful information about yourself; what you like and don't like, what works for you and what doesn't work. Dating also gives you lots of opportunities to speak up about what doesn't work for you, and if you are divorced, this is probably something you could use some practice with. Dating gives you lots of chances to say "no thank you" to people when a relationship isn't working for you, without feeling like you have to make up a lot of extraneous excuses. Ending a relationship because it's not working for you is the only reason you need to end a relationship, and when you get down to it, it's really the only reason people end relationships.

Keep in mind that the goal of dating is to one find one person you think you might have a future with (unless you are looking for multiple partners, but that's a subject for another book). I find getting to know one person at a time intimately to be all the challenge I need. The thought of doing that with two or more people at the same time is overwhelming. When you find someone you like, someone you think you may have a future with, let them know you want to have an exclusive relationship so that you can see if there is a future.

Avrum G. Weiss, Ph.D.

Chapter 2

For Men: How To Tell if She's Really Into You

Hint: The answer is a lot closer than you think.

Stereotypically, women pay more attention than men to how things are going in their relationships. Men stereotypically don't worry as much about how their relationships are going, and if they do, there is a lot of social pressure not to admit it. Men typically acknowledge insecurity about their relationships only when their girlfriend/partner withdraws in some way, such as not showing as much interest in what he is talking about, to losing interest in sex, or threatening to leave.

Once a man believes abandonment is a possibility he typically goes from zero to sixty in a heartbeat, becoming obsessively interested in how the relationship is going– buying gifts, taking his girlfriend/partner out for dinner, wanting to hear about her day, buying self-help books and suggesting they read them together, or even proposing the previously dreaded couples therapy.

Contrary to popular opinion, men are just as anxious as women about whether they are liked and accepted or at risk of being abandoned. It makes good sense to watch carefully and worry about any part of your life that so profoundly influences so much of your happiness. In reading this article you've taken the first step in acknowledging that you, just like every other man, have some anxiety about whether or not the woman you're involved with approves of you.

When a man is interested in figuring out how his relationship is going, he may ask his girlfriend/partner for reassurance. Of course, he will ask indirectly in a code that both of them understand perfectly well, because he is loath to acknowledge any insecurity directly to her. So, he'll ask, "Are you OK?" or "Is everything OK?"

Because he is feeling anxious and insecure, his girlfriend/partner's answers are never more than briefly satisfying, so he may escalate the frequency of his requests for reassurance to a maddening pace. Because no amount of reassurance ever soothed anyone's insecurity more than briefly, he doesn't really believe her answers, and concocts a whole series of credulity straining explanations for why she might be lying to him, like, "She's just a nice person and doesn't want to hurt my feelings."

Since none of her answers are ever convincing, he may decide that the only way to know her true, hidden feelings is to be like a detective and start looking for hidden evidence of how she really feels. He starts watching his girlfriend/partner carefully, hanging on the significance of any word spoken or not spoken, any action taken or not taken, searching for any sign of unhappiness or lack of interest. She hasn't mentioned where she wants to go on summer vacation this year, maybe she's not planning to be here? I notice she's starting to wear a ratty old tee shirt to bed at night, maybe she doesn't care if I find her attractive anymore? She's not asking as much about the big deal I've got going on at work, maybe she's losing interest in me?

Sadly, people generally find whatever they are looking for in another person.

If you go looking for evidence that your girlfriend/partner doesn't really like you, chances are you'll find it. You may even end up creating something that didn't previously exist, because approaching a relationship from a suspicious place inevitably creates more distance in the relationship.

I would like to suggest two steps to understanding how things are going in your relationship, each of which is a lot easier than playing detective and a lot more satisfying. The first step is to start by paying attention to your own experience rather than trying to figure out what's going on with your girlfriend/partner. Let yourself know what you know. It's not really much help to know if things are going well for her if they're not going well for you.

- How do you feel when you are with her?
- Do you enjoy yourself?
- Do you feel relaxed, comfortable being yourself, or more on edge, and worrying about pleasing her?

Once you figure out how you feel, then you can start making this a two-person equation.

No matter how hard you try, you are never going to be able to figure out what's going on in a relationship by yourself. You only have half the data; all you can do is extrapolate from the information you do have and your conclusions will mostly be off base, sometimes wildly so.

Relationships are mutual.

If things are working well for you, chances are they're going pretty well for her, too. On the other hand, if there are parts of the relationship that are not going well, then perhaps you could have a conversation about that.

It's surprising how often it doesn't even occur to people to have a mutual conversation about their relationship, or if it does occur to them, how intimidating the idea is. This is different from asking your partner for reassurance. I'm suggesting initiating a mutual conversation with your partner about how you each are feeling about the relationship. Questions like:

- *How are we doing? rather than Are you OK?*

- *Are you getting what you want and need from this relationship?*

- *Are there ways that I can be a better partner to you?*

- *How are you thinking about our relationship? Do you think we have a future?*

Many men, perhaps you too, have insecurities, and are anxious about being liked and approved of. Rather than trying to manage those insecurities by looking for answers outside of themselves, they could find that far more satisfying answers are a lot closer than they think; in themselves.

Part Two

Communication

By far, the most common reason that couples give for starting therapy together is problems in communication. "But I Am Listening to You" describes three levels of listening that can help people feel more fully heard and understood. "But I Was Just Being Honest" suggests that couples practice "relationally responsible speech," taking full responsibility for the impact of the words they use with each other.

Chapter 3

"But I *Am* Listening to You"

Being a good listener is important for any relationship. Here are three different types of listening.

At some point in most couples' arguments, one person is likely to complain to the other, "You're not listening to me!" It is most often the woman in heterosexual couples who has this complaint, and the man is often genuinely puzzled by her grievance. He will often summarize what she's just said as proof that he has, in fact, been listening, and is then even more confused when she continues to insist that he is still not listening. Clearly, they have differing understandings of the word "listen." He understands listening rather literally, meaning that he is listening to the words she is saying. She is using the word listening, but what she really wants is to feel understood. Knowing about three kinds of listening can help both partners learn how to listen in a way that helps the other to feel more fully understood.

Talking to yourself is not nearly as satisfying as talking to someone else, particularly if that person makes it clear that they get you, they understand. Listening is one of the most powerful yet underappreciated ways to feel closer with someone.

On the surface, listening seems so simple, something everyone knows how to do, and that we all do every day without thinking. At the same time, we are aware of subtleties in listening, because we think of some people as "good listeners" or "easy to talk to."

I want to talk about three types of listening; listening to content, listening between the lines, and listening relationally, which means simultaneously paying attention to your own thoughts and feelings as you listen.

Listening to the Content

This is the most basic kind of listening, the type of listening we do most of the time, the type of listening that people are referring to when they protest, "But I am listening to you!" While this kind of listening may seem relatively straightforward, even listening on this simplest level requires some skill and focus on the listener's part.

It is actually quite challenging to listen to another person talk about their experience without automatically translating it into our own frame of reference. In an all-too-common example, a woman starts talking to her husband/partner about something that is bothering her. Listening from his own frame of reference, the man hears his wife/partner bringing him a problem that she wants his help solving, so he starts offering suggestions. From the wife/partner's frame of reference, she is talking about something that is troubling her and just wants her husband/partner to hear her. Every time he offers a solution, she feels not heard. The husband/partner is incredulous when his wife/partner tells him he is not listening, because not only is he listening carefully to his wife/partner, he is trying everything he can think of to be helpful.

One concrete suggestion I offer to couples about listening is this: When your partner wants to talk to you about something, start the conversation by asking him or her how you can be helpful. *Would you like me to help you problem-solve this situation, or is this a case where you mostly want to feel understood and supported by me?* This may feel awkward for a while, but you will be surprised at how many times it will prevent arguments.

Listening Between the Lines

Imagine how frustrating it would be to talk with someone who simply parroted back everything you said. Research suggests that only about twenty percent of what we understand from others comes from what they say, so when we just listen to the content we are missing about 80% of what someone is trying to tell us. Feeling truly heard only happens when we also work to listen between the lines, which involves hearing the emotions underlying the content.

For example, imagine a friend talking to you about a new job she's applying for. She is talking about feeling insecure about whether she can get the job, and being too scared to let herself get excited and risk disappointment. You hear the content of what your friend is saying, but also notice a sense of excitement about her; her eyes are wide open, she is speaking rapidly, leaning forward, and despite how hard she is trying to convince herself otherwise, she does sound excited. You might say to your friend, "You know it's funny, you are talking about being scared and unsure of yourself, but I keep getting the sense that you are excited, too." You will probably find your friend will feel truly heard in a much deeper way that encourages her to explore the feelings of excitement that she has been reluctant to let herself feel. It is also likely that listening in this way will help the two of you feel much closer to each other.

Listening Relationally

The third type of listening involves paying attention to your own experience while also listening to someone else. Most people believe that being a good listener means that they have to ignore their own thoughts and feelings in order to really focus on what the other person is saying. The problem is that's not really possible. The best we can do is to pretend, and that can be very confusing to the person speaking.

Let us go back to the example of a friend talking to you about a job she has applied for. This time, imagine that you have been unemployed for six months. As you listen to your friend, your own experience keeps pushing into your awareness. You are scared you will not find a job, you are worried about losing your home, and the financial stress is affecting your marriage and your relationship with your kids. You're jealous of your friend and angry with her for talking about her good news without considering how it will affect you.

If you don't say anything to your friend about your experience as a listener, your friend will still sense that something is going on with you, and in the absence of any information from you, she will draw her own conclusions with the information available. She may conclude that you don't care about her, or that you think this is the wrong job for her, or she is not being a good friend to you. If, however, you share something of what is going on with you, the two of you may be able to talk through what is going on between you in a way that frees you up to be a better listener and a better friend. Learning how to listen relationally is the most effective way to help those you care about feel truly heard and understood, and the most powerful way to deepen your connection with others.

Chapter 4

"But I Was Just Being Honest!"

How to talk responsibly to someone you love.

Low many times have you had your feelings hurt by people speaking to you in the name of "telling the truth." Comments such as, "I think you've put on a little bit of weight" or "you're so controlling" or "you care more about your work than you do me," or other hurtful and insensitive comments have all been made in the name of "telling the truth."

In The United States, we place such a strong, sometimes overriding value on free speech that we may uphold an individual's right to say whatever she or he wants even when it is clearly harmful or intended to be harmful to the larger community. For example, the Supreme Court of the United States upheld the rights of the American Nazi Party to hold a march in Skokie, Illinois despite the fact that the march was targeted at a largely Jewish community and designed to inflict the most harm possible.

While we can debate the pros and cons of this approach as national policy, there is no doubt that the same approach does not work well at all in any kind of relationship. Words are very powerful. The biblical version of creation is that God created the world with words, "the word of God brought everything into being: heaven and earth, mountains and rivers, and every living thing" (Issacs). Words in relationships are also very powerful, with equal potential for helping or harming those we care most about. Couples clearly understand the power of words in their relationships, because when they decide to seek help from a therapist they usually describe their problem as "communication problems."

In relationships, rather than the one-sided valuing of free speech that we uphold as a nation, it is far more helpful to aspire to the feminist value of "relationally responsible speech." Speech that is relationally responsible is speech that takes responsibility for the impact of your words on the person you are talking to. When someone protests that they are "just telling the truth," they are defending their intent as benign or even helpful, and are indignant at being held accountable for the impact of their words, even if that impact could reasonably have been anticipated. They are being insensitive in the true meaning of the word, which is to "show no feelings or concerns for another's feelings."

Relationally responsible speech means the speaker considers the impact of his or her words, and then takes responsibility for the impact of those words, even if the impact is different from what she or he intended.

Returning to our earlier examples, the people speaking defend their speech by claiming a higher priority on "the truth" than the feelings of the people they are talking to. The problem with this argument is that they are not, in fact, telling the truth. It's not that they are inaccurate, or mistaken, or even dishonest. They are not telling the truth because it's not possible to speak about someone else's truth, only your own. What they are doing is simply speaking aloud some of the critical judgments they hold about the person they are speaking to. The only real truth we can tell is the truth about our own experience.

Let's take the example of one person accusing another of being "so controlling." It may or may not be true that the accused person is controlling; that's not for the accuser to say. The only truth that the accuser can talk about with complete authority is the truth of his or her own experience, such as, "when you talk to me the way you are now, it makes me feel bad, like there's no room for me in this conversation."

In the second example in which one person accuses another of "caring more about your work than me," again, the accuser can't possibly know the internal state of the accused. What the accuser can know with certainty is how this behavior makes him or her feel, as in, "when you come home this late, I start to feel very lonely, and it's hard for me to hold onto knowing that you care about me."

People sometimes add the phrase "I feel that" to the beginning of a sentence to disguise their critical intent and make it sound like they are talking about the truth of their own experience. However, "I feel like you care more about work than you do about me" is just the wolf of a judgment disguised in the sheep's clothing of a feeling word.

An interesting example of how complex these matters can be is when one person in a relationship has an affair. If the affair has truly ended, and the offending partner emerges from the affair clearer than ever about his commitment to his marriage, should he tell his wife about the affair just because that is the truth? Should he consider whether it would be better for their marriage to tell the truth or keep it to himself? If he decides it would be better for the marriage not to tell his wife, can the two of them truly have an intimate relationship with one of them holding such a secret?

The counter-argument is often made that restricting the way one talks is not natural, not spontaneous, and that intimacy requires people to talk openly and spontaneously with each other. It is true that to consider the impact of one's words before speaking is less spontaneous and less natural. So is not quitting your job when you have a bad day, or not hitting your children when you're angry at them, or not eating all the ice cream when you open the pint.

The last thing I want to discuss is "telling the truth" about your relationship to someone else you are close to. When you've had an argument with your partner/spouse, and things are not yet resolved, people often want to talk it over and get help from a friend. That can be a really good idea if you use these same relational principles in talking with your friend. It may seem that the way you talk about your spouse/partner to a friend won't matter as long as she or he doesn't know about it. I assure you that is not true. If you speak about your spouse/partner insensitively when talking to a friend, it has an impact similar to talking that way to your spouse/partner directly. I can't explain how that could be true, but I've seen it and experienced it enough times to know that it absolutely is true. If you seek out a friend to talk to who cares about your spouse/partner, and supports your relationship, and you speak in a way that is relationally responsible, in a way that you would not mind your partner/spouse hearing, that is very likely to be helpful to you and your spouse/partner in getting through this stuck place.

Part Three

Conflict

The real test of the durability of any relationship is not the strength of the initial attraction or how well the two people communicate, but how satisfactorily they resolve conflict. Conflict is an inevitable part of any intimate relationship. We all have a variety of ways that we seek to minimize or avoid conflict because it's uncomfortable and can threaten the security of the relationship. However, avoiding conflict inevitably leads to increasing distance and unhappiness in a relationship, and learning how to resolve conflict is one of the primary ways that people learn to be closer and more intimate.

Chapter 5

Why Do Men Get Nervous
When Women Get Emotional?

*How men's fear of mutual emotional exchanges
keeps them from the intimacy they truly want.*

Men generally get very nervous whenever women have strong feelings. It doesn't matter if she is scared, or sad, or angry, or even really happy. Even when women make it absolutely clear that they are not upset with their partner/husband, he'll probably still feel anxious. To manage their own anxiety, men often try to reassure women when they are emotional, or step in quickly to "fix" whatever is bothering them, or convince them that they don't have a good reason to be this upset; anything they can think of to calm women down.

For a lot of guys, their partner's distress becomes the single most important thing going on, and absolutely not much else can happen until that gets taken care of.

Why is a woman being openly so destabilizing emotionally for so many men? Why not just ignore her and go off and do your own thing until she's over it? Why do so many men find women's emotions impossible to ignore? As with most things having to do with relationships, the answer is pretty complicated.

Women getting emotional during an argument is particularly problematic for most men. Men tend to be more comfortable with facts than feelings. When an argument gets more emotional, men can feel uncharacteristically disadvantaged, like they are playing an away game on their wife/partner's home field.

Men often try to "win" arguments by going on the offensive, telling their wives/partners that they are "being hysterical" or pushing them to "calm down and make sense," trying to keep things focused on their home field of facts and practical matters and doing their best to keep all emotions out of it.

Even when their wife/partner's emotions have nothing to do with them, men can still feel compelled to curtail those emotions because they are raised to feel responsible for women's happiness. If women are unhappy about something, men are raised to believe that they have failed in some way. You can see how this leads to repetitive power struggles. Women often feel that they can't make the kind of intimate connection they are looking for with their husbands/partners. They quickly learn that if they show a little distress, he will immediately start to lean in and pay more attention.

While this is initially effective, after a while the guy is less responsive to his wife/partner's distress, so she has to escalate her expression of emotion, which is again effective for a while, until it's not, and things keep escalating from there.

Another reason that men are so bothered by women's strong feelings is that men secretly feel emotionally inadequate compared to their wives/partners.

On some level, most men recognize that they are not as emotionally well developed as their wives/partners. Their wives/partners seem to have stronger emotions, have an easier time expressing their feelings, and seem to be more empathetic in responding to other people's feelings. On a deeply unconscious level, many men are scared that there is something wrong with them when they don't have the kinds of emotional responses they see in their wives/partners.

My father died when I was a young man. I loved my father and was very close to him and decided I wanted to give his eulogy. My biggest fear was not that I wouldn't be able to get through it, but that I would not cry, which would confirm my worst fear about myself: that I was a cold, heartless son-of-a-bitch. I sobbed so much during the eulogy that the Rabbi repeatedly tried to pull me away from the lectern. Although distraught, I also felt an enormous sense of relief.

Interestingly, Freud theorized that when little girls saw their brother's or father's penis they would feel penis envy and judge themselves to be inadequate. On the other hand, little boys witness their mother's and sister's open display of emotions a lot more than little girls see a penis, yet it doesn't seem to have occurred to Freud that those boys might feel emotional envy and judge themselves to be emotionally inadequate.

Related to this feeling of inadequacy is the fear that comes from understanding that strong feelings are contagious. Being around other people who are expressing strong feelings is as contagious as a yawn. When women are more emotional, men are likely to feel internal stirrings of some of the feelings they have been taught to suppress. This is generally not a process that men are consciously aware of, they just know that they are getting increasingly uncomfortable and want to do whatever they can to get it to stop.

When men do feel uncomfortable in the face of women's strong feelings, there are three escalating levels of defense mechanisms they typically use.

DEFCON 1

Most men's first line of defense is to clamp down even tighter on their own emotional suppression. This strategy allows them to maintain at least a superficial connection with their partners while controlling the level of their own emotional activation.

DEFCON 2

If the level of emotional activation is still more than a man is comfortable tolerating, he can move to the next level, which is to withdraw. This strategy costs a man the level of connection he would prefer to maintain, but if he is emotionally activated enough, the safety of withdrawal may be worth it.

DEFCON 3

If emotional withdrawal and detachment are still not enough to soothe a man's own feelings, he can go on the offensive and try to silence women by criticizing them for being "too emotional" or "not rational". Men hold themselves up as the model for women to follow; logical, rational and, most importantly, in control of their feelings. The paradox is terribly frustrating to men: the more they withdraw or try to suppress women's emotional expression, the bigger those feelings get.

While these three defenses can be effective in keeping men from feeling flooded with their own feelings, they also clearly interfere with the kind of mutual emotional exchanges that can lead to the kind of intimacy we all want.

Chapter 6

Who Gets Up in the Middle of the Night in Your House?

On power struggles between men and women

about anxiety.

My wife abruptly woke me early this morning, shaking me and yelling, "What's that?"

As I groggily came to, I heard the noise she was referring to and reassured her that it was the sound of a window fan, then got up and turned it off. I was immediately angry at having my sleep so rudely interrupted for something that seemed trivial to me. I wondered why something that was bothering her ended up with me out of bed and awake and her going back to sleep? I quickly realized that she woke me up because she was scared and that both of us reflexively expected me to be in charge of fixing things that frightened her.

I woke in the morning with several questions on my mind:

- *Why did the noise bother my wife so much more than it bothered me? It's not just that she sleeps more soundly. My wife's default assumption was that there was something wrong, whereas mine was that everything was OK.*

- *Why did my wife automatically turn to me to take care of her anxiety? I'm pretty sure she did not consider getting up to investigate herself, yet if she were alone I'm sure she would have taken care of it.*

- *Why did I automatically assume that it was my job to take care of her anxiety?*

Anxiety in its simplest form is a preoccupation with a series of fearful predictions about an imagined future. Anxiety is not only normal, but it is, to an extent, adaptive, alerting us to potential dangers. Mild to moderate amounts of anxiety increase productivity.

In our culture, women tend to be more anxious than men (Remes, et al., 2016). Because men hold more privilege, things in general work better for them. Men face less challenge, less struggle, and less uncertainty in their lives than women. In other words, men have less to be anxious about. Women have less privilege. They are biologically tied to their offspring, are at more risk of abandonment than their male partners, earn 30% less, and are more likely to live in poverty if divorced. Accordingly, women have good reason to be anxious.

Anxiety is also contagious and it's relational, meaning that when one person in a relationship feels more anxiety, the other is likely to feel less. For example, one person in a couple might wake up in the middle of the night, feeling anxious and not be able to get back to sleep. She wakes her partner and talks to him about what she's feeling anxious about, whereupon she goes right back to sleep and now he feels her anxiety and can't go back to sleep (Felder, 1988). When women carry more than their share of anxiety in a relationship, it protects men from feeling their own anxiety. Women have it and don't want it. Men have less of it, or at least are not willing to let themselves know they have it, and don't want to catch it from their partners.

Women naturally want to spread the load, they want men to feel some of the anxiety they are carrying, and men are naturally resistant. For men, being around women who are anxious often makes them feel more of their own anxiety, which their privilege has largely protected them from experiencing. Men are socialized to think of anxiety as a feminine trait, and taught to hide their anxiety and "never let them see you sweat," in large part to protect their privileged status. As a result, men do their best to "take care" of women and "solve" women's anxiety in order to protect themselves from feeling more anxious.

Women, in turn, are socialized to be more openly anxious with their male partners because it's often one of the few effective ways of getting some of the emotional attention and caring that they otherwise find difficult to obtain. This often results in a mutually dissatisfying polarization in heterosexual couples in which the woman takes on the role of the anxious person and the man the role of the person responsible for managing his wife's/partner's anxiety.

All of this helps explains why my wife was more worried about the strange sound in the middle of the night than I was, and why we both automatically assumed that I would be the one to get out of bed to investigate. The way out of this polarized relationship pattern is for each person in the relationship to expand his or her capacity to experience the role they are blocked from. For men, this might involve not working so hard to suppress their partner's anxiety and allowing themselves to feel more of their own anxiety. For women, this might mean not relying on using anxiety to make a connection with their partners and, instead, addressing their frustrations and desire for more emotional connection more directly.

Chapter 7

Why Does Conflict Escalate Between Men and Women?

Could the answer be avoidant men

and anxious women?

A couple are having an argument, the woman is hurt and angry. Her husband/partner can clearly see she's upset, and her tears make him surprisingly uncomfortable. While he would like to feel empathy, there is something about her strong feelings that is distressing to him and gets in the way. Because he is uncomfortable with his own strong feelings, the man begins to emotionally withdraw and detach to protect himself. For reasons he doesn't fully understand, it becomes increasingly important to him to remain rational and unemotional, and he is increasingly critical of, and irritated with, his wife for being "too emotional."

The wife can feel her husband withdrawing, and the more he withdraws, the more anxious she becomes and the more urgently she pursues him to find a way to make some kind of emotional connection with him.

Now, they are locked in a mutually destructive cycle; the more she pushes for the emotional connection she yearns for, the more he detaches. The more he tries to control his own fear by detaching, the more anxious she gets.

One way of understanding these escalating dynamics is through the lens of attachment theory.

Attachment theory suggests the quality of a child's emotional attachment to his or her early caregivers sets the pattern for how that child will respond to perceived hurt, separations, or threats in adult love relationships. To oversimplify:

• *If your early caregivers were consistently available and attended to your needs, it is likely that you will be securely attached. Securely attached people are attracted to intimacy as adults and are not prone to worry a lot about conflict or temporary breaches of connection.*

• *If your early caregivers were inconsistently available and unpredictable in the ways they attended to your needs, you may be anxiously attached. People who are anxiously attached crave intimacy and closeness but worry a lot about conflict or anything else that suggests a potential break in connection.*

• *If your early caregivers were generally inattentive and did not do a very good job of attending to your needs, you may be avoidantly attached. People who are avoidantly attached feel uncomfortable with too much closeness and may even see closeness as a threat.*

Research suggests (Gottman, 2015) that seventy percent of the difficulties in heterosexual relationships are caused by men who are avoidantly attached being partnered with women who are anxiously attached. The man in the example above could be thought of as avoidantly attached. His wife/partner's open expression of emotions is more intimate than he is comfortable with, so he modulates his own feelings with his preferred strategy of withdrawing. The woman in the example could be thought of as anxiously attached. Her partner's withdrawal confirms her worst fears of being abandoned and escalates her level of emotional distress. What she needs most terrifies him.

In these relationships, when women's interest in connection and intimacy is not met by their partners, it puts those women in a vulnerable, one down position. The less powerful person is inevitably in the demanding position, pushing for change in the relationship that would put them on a more equal footing. Since men benefit from the emotional status quo in the relationship, they withdraw to resist any change.

The way out of this escalating conflict is for each partner to claim aspects of the other's position in order to depolarize the couple. For men, this means relinquishing some of the privilege inherent in the withdrawn, avoidant position and allowing themselves to be more aware of, and then risking acknowledging some of their own needs for intimate connection, and their dependency on their wives/partners.

Chapter 8

Relationship Repair 101

Five things everyone needs to feel better

after a fight.

Couples often avoid conflict both because they are uncomfortable with it and because they are not confident about their relationship repair skills and worry that repeated conflict will create more distance in the relationship. However, conflict is not generally what tears couples apart. Conflict is inevitable in any intimate relationship. The only way to avoid conflict is to avoid intimacy. How often a couple fight is not what makes or breaks a relationship, it's how couples resolve conflict that is most important in a relationship.

When we are hurt in a relationship, there are five things we need to feel better.

First and foremost, we need the person who has hurt us to understand our hurt feelings. Having them just repeat the story back to us doesn't do the trick. We need them to let us know that they understand how we feel, and how their behavior has affected us. "I get that what I said to you was very hurtful and really made you question how much I care about you, and how sensitive I am to how you feel."

After knowing that our partner understands how we feel, the next thing we need to know is that they care about how we feel. This is best communicated by telling the person you've hurt something about how you feel about hurting them, something about your own empathetic emotional response to their hurt. "It makes me feel awful when I hear how my words affected you. I hate the thought that you can't count on knowing how I feel about you."

Ideally, the person who hurt you would have done some reflection about what was going on with them and why they behaved in such a hurtful way. It's helpful for them to tell you something about where he was coming from, why it seemed OK to behave the way they did, and what their intent was. "I think I was insensitive to you because I've been upset with you about something else for a while now and haven't found a way to talk to you about it." If you can gain some understanding about where he was coming from, it helps make the next step more believable.

The last step is letting the person you hurt know what steps you are willing to take to avoid hurting them in this way again. This step is more believable if you've already let her know that you have some insight into what was going on for you. Without that, it is unlikely that you will be able to avoid repeating the same hurtful pattern. "I think if I commit to a time when we regularly check in with each other about how we are doing together as a couple, it would be easier for me to keep current with you and not hold onto resentments.

While these five steps seem relatively simple, that does not necessarily make them easy. They'll work well when you and your partner are trying to work through fairly straight-forward issues. On the other hand, any area in which you or your partner are particularly sensitive or feel more vulnerable will be trickier. If you keep trying these steps and repeatedly end up in the same painful place, I hope you will consider getting someone to help you navigate the more challenging waters.

Chapter 9

What's All That Fussing and Fighting?

How men can look forward to arguing with their partners.

If you think makeup sex is something that only happens in the movies, this chapter is for you.

It is not uncommon in my work as a psychotherapist to talk to men who have become so conflict-avoidant that placating their wives is the most important thing in the relationship to them. They are so scared of their partners' disapproval they've essentially given up on any efforts to try to work things out or get closer. All they want now is for her to stop being mad at them.

> "Like most guys I would rather face the muzzle of an assault rifle than a pissed off wife."
>
> — *Wild Fire* by Nelson Demille

Interestingly, men are not only often comfortable with conflict in other settings, they sometimes even seek it out. Sports is a good example, and even the workplace can provide opportunities for enjoyable conflict. The most important difference between conflict in intimate relationships and conflict in these other settings is that the goal is completely different.

In sports or the workplace, the goal is to win, to defeat your opponent. So when your opponent gets angry or aggressive, it is often appropriate and effective to match or exceed their level of anger or aggression if your goal is to defeat them. In intimate relationships, not so much. Defeating your partner in an intimate relationship is not a satisfying outcome for many people.

In intimate relationships, anger is simply an indication that the other person doesn't like the way things are going in the relationship and would like for things to be better. If your wife says to you, "I'm angry that you forgot we agreed to work on the yard this weekend and you made other plans," that's not an attack or a personal criticism that needs to be defended, or worse, retaliated against. She didn't say that you did anything wrong, or that you need to do anything different. She just said she didn't like the way things went between you. She's giving you important information about how she feels about her connection to you, and your job is just to listen.

Of course, in the real world, anger is rarely delivered quite so cleanly. The message you get may sound more like "I'm angry at you for making other plans, and you always do that because I'm not as important to you as your friends!" In this case, your job is still to listen, although you may have to listen a little harder between the lines to get to the important information. Good conflict helps people resolve issues and feel closer.

That's why people get excited about makeup sex; couples often feel much closer after a good argument, and there's an excitement that comes from having cleared the air that can energize the couple sexually.

Not all conflict is helpful.

Conflict can also be abusive, which calls for an entirely different set of responses. Abuse is not about trying to get closer to another person. Abuse is speaking without regard for the impact of your words on another person, or in the extreme, even intentionally trying to hurt another person. The appropriate response to abuse is to set firm limits, and if that doesn't work, to leave.

Tell your partner that you are going to leave for a little while until things calm down between you. Tell her how long you will be gone and be clear that you would like to continue the conversation when you are both able, and not just push it under the rug.

Women often get angry when they want more closeness and connection with their partners. Since men are socialized to feel responsible for any unhappiness in their partners, they often hear her request for more intimacy as a complaint, or even an indictment that they have done something wrong, or are lacking in some important way. They react to what they hear as criticism by being defensive, frustrating their partners even further by creating more rather than less distance . . .and off they go.

Here are a few tips to help you have the kind of positive conflict that can help couples resolve conflict and feel closer:

Intention

Be intentional about your arguments. Arguments should be a way of working things out so that you can get closer. Think about the ways in which you want to feel closer to your partner and keep that in the front of your mind during the argument.

Timing

Pick a time and place where you can both be at your best. This is tricky stuff, there is no need to make it harder by arguing when you are both tired or will be interrupted. Pick a time and a place to talk where you can concentrate on each other and won't be interrupted. I always forget that I have to say this to people but turn off the television and your cell phones!

No harsh startups

Noted couples researcher John Gottman (2015) found that when arguments don't start well, they are likely to go badly. If the argument gets off to a harsh start and looks like it's going South quickly, don't be afraid to put it on pause and come back to it another time.

Your perspective

Talk about yourself and what you are feeling, rather than making attributions about your partner. Everyone is defensive about someone trying to criticize or correct them, it's just not going to go well. If you don't like the way your partner is behaving, talk about how that behavior impacts you, rather than telling her why her behavior is wrong.

Speak responsibly.

Think about the impact of your words before you speak them. Take responsibility for the impact of your words, even if the impact of your words was different from what you intended. In Jewish ethics, harmful speech is a greater sin than theft because if you steal from someone you can make reparations, but you cannot undo the harm caused by speech.

My hope is that using some of these tips will not only help you not dread arguing with your partner, but also help you to feel more confident that facing conflict head on will help the two of you to feel closer.

Chapter 10

Men: Why Apologizing Won't Get You Out of the Doghouse

Four steps to effective relationship repair.

As a psychotherapist, the most common complaint I hear from men who are partnered with a woman is that she is unceasingly critical of him. Men talk about never being able to get it right and not understanding what the rules are, or if there even are any rules. Men tend to approach this problem somewhat concretely, working stubbornly to understand what they're doing wrong so they can prevent further disapproval. At the same time, most men do have some understanding that their wives/partners are not primarily dissatisfied with their behavior but with their being inattentive and emotionally insensitive.

Stereotypically, when a man's wife/partner is upset with him, it is referred to as "being in the doghouse."

The punishment for men's transgressions most often consists of women withholding attention and affection, emotional withdrawal, "giving him the cold shoulder," both because that's most often the only power women have in heterosexual relationships and because women understand how vulnerable their male partners are to any threat of emotional abandonment.

The doghouse is about much more than just withholding sex, although one stereotypical punishment is getting sent to sleep on the couch. It's about withholding attention, validation, conversation, and connection; all the things that men would probably not even know they need until their wives/partners withhold them.

This dynamic is a rebalancing of power in the relationship, with women using the only means available---a passive punishing withholding---to reassert whatever small share of power they have in the relationship. There is typically no meaningful conversation or attempt to work things through. The man is simply punished until his wife is ready to end the punishment. He is, of course, always vulnerable to being sent back to the doghouse.

Retailer JCPenney released an advertisement called "The doghouse" (JC Penny, 2008), which cautions men against buying the wrong gifts for their wives. In the ad, a man offends his wife by giving her an expensive vacuum cleaner for their anniversary. She marches him outside to a doghouse and instructs him to "get inside." The man enters and falls into a purgatory in which a group of men are perpetually folding laundry. The man protests that, "I don't deserve to be here. I didn't do anything," and another man tells him that, "Every man in the doghouse thinks he's innocent." This ad was viewed 1.7 million times in the first three weeks.

Since men superficially misunderstand conflict with their wives/partners as a behavioral problem, they tend to seek behavioral solutions, typically, an apology. Apologies are not generally effective relationship repair, because they are most often a thinly veiled attempt to prematurely bring the argument to a close and restore the status quo without ever giving a full hearing to their wives/partners feelings.

On the other hand, if men understood conflict with their wives/partners as a problem in the relationship rather than their own individual failing, they would have a much better chance of understanding what they need to do to repair a relationship. For more mutually satisfying conflict resolution, I suggest that men start with a 30-day apology moratorium. Begin by not apologizing for anything for 30 days, it may help you to listen more.

Listening more will set the stage for the four steps outlined below to help you and your partner feel more confident about handling conflict in your relationship.

1. *When your wife/partner is hurt, the first thing she needs to know is that you understand how she feels, on her terms, not yours. This is not just a matter of repeating back to her what she said. Men sometimes get angry and frustrated when parroting back their wives'/partners' words doesn't smooth things over, complaining, "but I am listening to you!" One of the biggest mistakes men make in relationships is stopping there. Nobody feels heard or knows that you care if you just repeat back what they said. You have to also listen between the lines, use your intuition to go beyond the*

concrete words and get the deeper sense of what she is talking about.

2. *The second and more important step, and the one that people sadly often leave out, is to take responsibility for the impact of your behavior. This does not mean saying you were wrong. It's not about right or wrong. It's about acknowledging that you understand how your behavior has impacted someone you love. Whether or not you meant to hurt her is largely irrelevant, and falling back on that is just a way to dodge acknowledging that you hurt someone.*

3. *Your partner needs to know that hurting her matters to you, that you have some personal reaction to her being hurt, and that it has some impact on you. You have to be willing to put a little skin in the game, dig a little deeper in yourself and share with her some of how you are feeling in response to her feelings. This is what empathy is.*

4. *Lastly, you have to be willing to give her some realistic indication of what you are willing to do to decrease the likelihood of hurting her in this way in the future. Don't promise you won't do it again because you almost certainly will. Most of the significant hurts in couples come from people acting out their own deeply ingrained characterological patterns. Much as you might try, it is highly unlikely that you are going to be able to change that overnight. It's not a measure of how much you care about someone, but of how deeply ingrained these patterns are. The fact is that we actually unconsciously choose a mate precisely because s/he is likely to play out these exact same*

Avrum G. Weiss, Ph.D.

patterns that are so hurtful to us, but that's a matter for yet another book.

What you can offer is some realistic understanding of where this behavior is coming from for you, and what kind of internal work you are willing to do to be more understanding and more sensitive to the impact of your behavior on her.

Part Four

Sex

Most people intuitively understand that sex is a very important part of intimate relationships. People tend to overvalue the importance of sex early in their relationships, and often undervalue its importance as the relationship progresses. A mutually satisfying sexual relationship is a vitally important part of maintaining an intimate connection. Good sex is like having healthy cartilage in your knee. When you have a good amount of cartilage everything goes pretty smoothly and you don't have to think a lot about how your knee works. When the cartilage starts to wear thin things can get pretty painful and what was spontaneous and easy going can start to feel forced and labored.

Chapter 11

It's Not Just About the Orgasm

How men use sex to reassure themselves

against the fear of being abandoned.

Women are often confused by their male partners' sense of urgency about sexual frequency. Men wanting a lot of sex is not surprising to women. We are all raised to believe that men have a stronger sex drive than women, but that a contextual stereotype does not take into account the multifaceted factors that comprise sexual desire (Nimbi, et al., 2019). What is surprising to women is the desperate sense of urgency they feel from their partners about sex. At times it's not just that their partners want sex, it's more like they need sex, almost as if it were a life and death matter.

Women are confused about men's sexuality because men don't let women know that sex is about a lot more than just having an orgasm. If it were just about the physical release then men who are partnered would simply masturbate as often as they liked and there wouldn't be this pervasive tension in heterosexual relationships about sexual frequency. One of the reasons that sex is so important to men is that because the homophobic prohibitions against men touching each other in any kind of intimate way mean that sex is often the only opportunity men have to intimately touch and be touched by another person. A member of my men's therapy group recently said that he looked forward to coming to the group every week over the years because the hugs the men in the group exchanged was the only touch he could count on all week. Single men in particular can go days, weeks, months or even years without any kind of intimate touch in their lives. While I hope that physical touch is something that you take for granted in your life, research has demonstrated that infants can literally die from a lack of touch alone (Frank, et al., 1996).

Men's sense of sexual urgency runs much deeper than just a need to be touched. Many men also harbor a deep-seated, largely unconscious fear of being abandoned by their female partners. While men do their best to hide this fear, it shows up in how conflict avoidant men can be in relationships, and how hard they will work to stay in their partner's good graces. "Happy wife, happy life." Men's fears of being abandoned can seem intractable at times, impervious to any words of reassurance from their partners. Sometimes it is only the physical intimacy of sex that can penetrate this resistance and help men feel truly loved and give a respite from the fear of being abandoned.

Because men are socialized not to show any signs of weakness or dependency, they often compartmentalize their sexuality, pretending that their desire for sex is simply the need for a physical release, and carefully hiding their powerful underlying emotional needs. This rather impersonal approach to sex is often not very appealing to their female partners, resulting in either outright rejection or at best a not very intimate sexual exchange which is not satisfying to either partner. The key to unlocking this dynamic is for men to learn how to talk to their female partners about their underlying needs for connection and fears of being abandoned, rather than acting those feelings out sexually. As men are able to talk more openly with their partners about their underlying emotional needs and fears, the couple is increasingly likely to learn a variety of new and more mutually satisfying ways of sharing intimate experiences together.

Chapter 12

What if He Can't?
What if She Doesn't?

How men's fear of sexual inadequacy

impacts their relationships.

Men are socialized to equate masculinity with self-confidence, to put up a good front and always present as self-assured, even when they are not. "Never let them see you sweat." Men are trained to think of life as a zero-sum game with winners and losers, so they attack any indication of a fear of inadequacy in another man as a sign of a weakness that can be exploited. As a result, men's fears of being inadequate go underground, hidden from themselves, from their partners, and from other men.

It's not surprising then that heterosexual men's fears of inadequacy show up most clearly in the intimate setting of the bedroom with women. Fears of erectile dysfunction are just the tip of the iceberg. Men's fears of inadequacy run all the way to the depths of questions such as whether he really is a man, or can ever be loved by a woman.

Stereotypically, men are thought to be self-centered and compartmentalized lovers (Diamond, 2017), more interested in the physical act of sex and their own pleasure than in an intimate connection with a partner. The extreme of this attitude is represented by a man who described his experience of sex as "masturbation with a woman in the general area." Men are also socialized to equate masculinity with a sexual desire so strong as to be indiscriminate (Diamond, 2017), i.e. that a real man is eager for sex anytime, anywhere, with anyone.

There is actually significant research that supports these stereotypes. Neuroscientists Ogas and Gaddam (2011) studied the internet porn viewing habits of millions of men around the world and came to the disturbing conclusion that "men's brains are designed to objectify females." Men's sexuality as revealed by their uncensored internet viewing preferences does tend to be compartmentalized, and what the authors call a "solitary affair" that can exist outside of the context of a relationship.

What is intriguing about this research is that what turned men on the most was depictions of intense sexual pleasure in women (Ogas & Gaddam, 2011). This confirms other surveys of men who said that pleasuring their partner was more important to them than their own pleasure. How can men be both self-centered lovers interested only in their own pleasure and be more focused on their partner's pleasure than their own? The paradox is readily resolved when we understand that men's focus on their partners' pleasure is only partially an act of generosity, and primarily an effort to stave off their own feelings of insecurity.

There is an old saying that women need to feel loved to want to have sex, and that men need to have sex to feel loved. Approaching a woman openly with your sexual desires is an inherently vulnerable act for men that often stirs up deep seated fears of inadequacy. Women are often surprised at the strength of their husband/partner's emotional response when turned down for sex, mistakenly attributing those reactions to misguided notions about the strength of men's libido.

Similarly, women often misunderstand men's request that they initiate sex more often as a simple request for more sex. When women are more open about their own sexual desires it frees men from the insecurity they often feel about being rejected, or more profoundly, from feeling not desirable or even not lovable. Men often feel like they are putting their entire sense of worth and self-acceptance on the line when they approach their partners sexually. Intercourse for men is a literal return to the insides of a woman's body, the place from whence they came, so it is a powerfully regressive experience, the ultimate reassurance of their acceptance and symbolically a powerful test of their self-worth.

Women's orgasms are equally important to men for similar reasons. Men report feeling more masculine when their partner has an orgasm (Chadwick, 2017). The more insecure a man feels about his masculinity, the more important it is to him that his partner have an orgasm. Women understand this and so have been known to fake orgasms to reassure their partners. One woman said, "if he doesn't think I had an orgasm, he won't give up, just keeps at me until I feel pressured" (Ley, 2017). It's clear that this kind of pressure is about more than generosity on the man's part. It is also a reflection of men's need to prove themselves to be adequate, worthy of being loved, and to forestall their fears of being abandoned.

As you would expect, men's fears of sexual inadequacy have a powerful effect on their relationships with their wives/partners. These fears may show up as inhibited sexual desire in men. In one study, 15% of men in long-term partnerships reported they had lost almost all interest in sex for a period of three months or longer in the past year (IFLS Science, 2017). This is not about aging, because the highest rate was in men aged 35-44.

Men's fears of being sexually inadequate also affect their relationships in more subtle ways. Noted sex therapist Esther Perel (2007) says that men's reliance on sex to reassure themselves about their larger sense of adequacy leads them to be so other-centered in sex that they are afraid that if they truly inhabit their bodies and surrender to the experience of their own pleasure for just a moment, that their partner will be hurt or angry, and will punish or even abandon them. As a result, women often complain that their partners are too tentative, that they approach them as if asking permission rather than expressing their desire.

Perel describes this as "a way of approaching . . . that doesn't say 'I want you' as much as 'Do you want me?'" Men are being careful, which is what they think they are supposed to do, but taken to extremes, this can be a turn off for women, more like a little boy asking for permission than a man expressing his desire for them.

The less aware of these fears men are, and the less the couple is able to talk about them, the greater the impact. The first step in helping couples is for both of them to develop a deeper understanding of the fears of inadequacy that men often struggle with, and finding ways to talk about them.

Part Five

Love

At last, we arrive at our ultimate destination; an enduring, mutually loving relationship. The last two articles of the anthology outline a mutual understanding of love and suggest an understanding of love as a behavior rather than an emotion.

Chapter 13

Why Men are Confused About "I Love You"

"I love you" means

"I love the me I am when I'm with you."

When I was a kid, my parents were very persnickety about language. For example, whenever I passionately declared that I "loved" catsup, one of my parents would be sure to correct me by asking, "are you going to marry catsup?" They were instructing me that the word "love" was reserved for the feelings a person has about a life partner and, therefore, not to be used for something as mundane as catsup. The problem with my parent's linguistic fanaticism was that they never suggested an alternative. "I really like catsup a lot" just didn't fully capture my passionate feelings about catsup.

A lot of straight men have this same problem in romantic relationships as adults. As a relationship progresses and their feelings mature and develop, a lot of men soon run out of words to describe how they feel. Just as when I was a kid, "I really like you a lot" doesn't seem quite adequate to describe the feeling someone hopes to have about the person they've been sleeping with for nine months. Telling their partner, "I love you" might seem like the next logical step, but those words are freighted with a lot of meanings in our culture that make both men and women hesitant to use them.

Because we only have the one word, "love," to describe such a wide range of feelings, and because, like my parents, we are socialized to equate love with marriage, many straight couples get stuck in a bit of a standoff about who is going to use the word first. Women are socialized to believe that marriage is something that women want and men don't, so they hesitate to say "I love you" for fear that their partner will hear this as a marriage proposal and run for the hills. Men are similarly socialized to believe that marriage is something that they won't like and should avoid for as long as possible. Men hesitate to use the words "I love you" for fear of giving the impression that it is only a matter of time before the ring follows.

Feminist theory offers men and women a way out of this bind.

In feminist theory, emotional experience is relational, meaning that emotions like love are not an experience that one person has alone, but are mutual experiences, experiences that are shared between two people. This approach immediately lets men off the hook. Men don't have to struggle in isolation, trying on their own to figure out the right word to describe how they feel about their partner. Love is an experience that is shared between two people. Whatever any man is feeling is just his own version of what two people in a relationship both feel. The two of them have to work together to figure out the right words to describe how they feel.

From a relational perspective, it is only through intimate relationships that we become most fully ourselves. Everyone has within them the potential for the full range of emotional experience. We are all capable of feeling everything, but that potential only comes fully alive in relationships. For example, I might think of myself as a person who does not get angry. No matter what the circumstances, I pride myself on never getting angry. However, if my wife announces one day that she's in love with another man, and is taking the children and moving to Alaska to be with him, I will hopefully discover that I actually do have the capacity to feel anger, just like everyone else does.

So it is with love.

Everyone has the capacity to love someone else; we only learn about that capacity in intimate relationships. One of the most wonderful things about love is that it makes you a bigger person, more fully yourself. From this perspective, men don't have to worry so much about whether or not to say "I love you," because love is not just a feeling you have about another person, but also a description of how you feel about yourself in a particular relationship. From this perspective, "I love you," really means, "I love myself when I'm with you," which should be a lot less threatening for men to say.

Chapter 14

Men Need To Understand Love Is a Behavior

Are you hooked on a feeling, or a behavior?

I saw an all-too-familiar but deeply disturbing sight the other day. I watched a young man standing in a light rain with his son, who seemed to be about six years old. The man was engrossed in texting on his phone, completely ignoring his son who was crying gently, plaintively telling his father that he was cold and wet and asking his dad to please pick him up and take him home. His father, without ever losing a moment's focus on his texting, reassured his son that, "It's OK buddy, daddy loves you, just give me a minute to finish this and we can go home."

It reminded me of all of the times I have sat in my office as a psychotherapist and listened to people describe the stunningly bad behavior they've tolerated at the hands of other people. When they see the spontaneous horrified look on my face, they often rush in to reassure me and perhaps themselves that, "It's OK, because I know they love me." At this point I am often speechless because they have just made it very clear that they are not interested in my questioning their conclusion that the abuse they are experiencing is an expression of love. It's as if they are reciting a mantra, "I know they love me," and the purpose of that mantra is to reinforce the dissociation that allows them to stay in place and tolerate harmful relationships.

"Personally, it has taken me 47 years to stop calling people who are mean to you, 'in love' with you."

— Uma Thurman

Love is a strange word, certainly one of the most confusing and complicated words in the English language. We say with great feeling that we "love" our local football team, and then use the same word with a lot less feeling to say that we "love" a great hamburger, and then even more confusingly use the exact same word to refer to the feeling we have for our children. Maybe we should be like the Inuits, who have 50 different variations of words for snow, and come up with a variety of words for the different kinds of love.

Since that seems unlikely, I have a simpler solution to propose. What if we considered love as a behavior rather than as a feeling. If love is a feeling, then it's hard to know when love is real because you have no way to know how someone is feeling. You can only infer how someone is feeling by how they act. Why not be more direct and just use the word love to refer to the behavior itself. Very simply, when someone is behaving lovingly towards you, that means they love you. If they are behaving badly towards you, then they don't love you.

The counter argument is that someone may be behaving badly towards you in the moment, but you know he loves you because he has behaved lovingly towards you other times. First of all, I would ask you to think back as honestly as you can about the ratio of the times he has behaved lovingly towards you vs. the times he has behaved badly before you characterize his overall behavior as loving. Even if you come up with a positive ratio, and he is not treating you well now, then we can conclude that he is not being loving towards you right now.

The advantage of thinking of love as a behavior rather than a feeling is that you will be fooled less often. When I played basketball, the coach always told us that on defense you should focus on the other guy's middle and not get distracted by what he does with the ball. The wisdom of this is that your opponent can fake one way with the ball and then go in another direction, but you can't fake with your middle. Whichever way your middle goes, the rest of you is sure to follow. In this case, our words are the potential ball fake, and our middle is our behavior. If we don't follow the ball we are less susceptible to ball fakes and more likely to see how someone's behavior is the clearest reflection of where their middle is headed.

#

Previously Published Components

1. https://goodmenproject.com/featured-content/shrinks-take-dating-wcz/

2. https://goodmenproject.com/featured-content/hey-guys-heres-how-to-tell-if-shes-really-into-you-wcz/

3. https://goodmenproject.com/featured-content/but-i-am-listening-to-you-wcz/

4. https://goodmenproject.com/featured-content/but-i-was-just-being-honest-wcz/

5. https://goodmenproject.com/featured-content/why-do-men-get-nervous-when-women-get-emotional-wcz/

6. https://goodmenproject.com/featured-content/who-gets-up-in-the-middle-of-the-night-lbkr/

7. https://goodmenproject.com/featured-content/why-does-conflict-escalate-between-men-and-women-wcz/

8. https://goodmenproject.com/featured-content/relationship-repair-101-wcz/

9. https://goodmenproject.com/featured-content/whats-all-that-fussing-and-fighting-wcz/

10. https://goodmenproject.com/featured-content/men-why-apologizing-wont-get-you-out-of-the-doghouse-wcz/

11. https://goodmenproject.com/featured-content/its-not-just-about-the-orgasm-wcz/

12. https://goodmenproject.com/featured-content/what-if-i-cant-what-if-she-doesnt-wcz/

13. https://goodmenproject.com/featured-content/why-men-are-confused-about-i-love-you-wcz/

14. https://goodmenproject.com/featured-content/love-is-a-behavior-wcz/

Alphabetical Index

Bibliography

Buber, M. (1937). *I and thou*. Edinburgh.

Chadwick, S. B., & van Anders, S. M. (2017). Do women's orgasms function as a masculinity achievement for men. *The Journal of sex research*, 54(9), 1141-1152.

Diamond, J. (2017). The one thing men want more than sex. *Good Men Project*.

Erikson, E. (1968). *Identity, Youth and Crisis*. New York: W.W. Norton.

Frank, D. A., Klass, P. E., Earls, F., & Eisenberg, L. (1996). Infants and young children in orphanages: one view from pediatrics and child psychiatry. Pediatrics, 97(4), 569–578.

Giorgi, A. (1988). *Psychology as a Human Science*. Addison Wesley.

Gottman, J. (2015). *The Seven Principles for Making Marriage Work: A Practical Guide From the Country's Foremost Relationship Expert*. Harmony.

Guntrip, H. (2018). *Schizoid phenomena, object relations and the self*. Routledge.

(2015). Harvard Second Generation Study of Adult Development. Retrieved November 27, 2018, from http://www.adultdevelopmentstudy.org.

Science, I. F. L. S. (2017). New Sexual Desire Survey Reveals Some Curious Differences Between Men And Women.

https://www.iflscience.com/health-and-medicine/new-sexual-desire-survey-reveals-curious-differences-between-men-women/all/.

Issacs, J. The Creation of the World. https://www.chabad.org/library/article_cdo/aid/246605/jewish/Creation-of-the-World.htm.

Jack, D. C. (1991). *Silencing the self: Women and depression.* Harvard University Press.

Penny, J. C. (2008). Beware of the doghouses. https://www.youtube.com/watch?v=Twivg7GkYts.

Joiner, T. (2015). *Lonely at the Top: the High Cost of Men's Success.* St. Martins Press.

Jordan, J. (2017). *Handbook of counseling women: 2nd edition.* Los Angeles: Saga.

Jordan, K., Kaplan, A., Stiver, I., Surrey, J., & Miller, J.B. (1991). *Women's Growth in Connection: Writings from the Stone Center.* New York: Guilford.

Kuhn, T. S. (1970). *The Structure of Scientific Revolutions.*

Kuhn, T. S. (1970). *The Structure of Scientific Revolutions* (2nd ed.). University of Chicago Press.

Levinson, D. J. (1978). *The Seasons of a man's life* (1st ed. ed.). New York: Knopf.

Ley, D. (2017). Why He Cares About Your Orgasm: Research sheds light on mens' motivation for giving pleasure. https://www.psychologytoday.com/us/blog/women-who-stray/201703/why-he-cares-about-your-orgasm.

Lyons-Ruth, K., Bureau, J.-F., Easterbrooks, M. A., Obsuth, I., Hennighausen, K., & Vulliez-Coady, L. (2013). Parsing the construct of maternal insensitivity: Distinct longitudinal pathways associated with early maternal withdrawal. *Attachment & Human Development*, 15(5-6), 562-582.

McAdams, D. P., Lester, R. M., Brand, P. A., McNamara, W. J., & Lensky, D. B. (1988). Sex and the TAT: Are women more intimate than men? Do men fear intimacy. *Journal of Personality Assessment*, 52(3), 397-409.

Moore, D. S. (2015). *The Developing Genome*. Oxford University Press, USA.

Morris, D. (1969). *The Naked Ape*. Dell Publishing Company.

O'neil, J. M. (2015). *Men's gender role conflict: Psychological costs, consequences, and an agenda for change*. American Psychological Association.

Ogas, O., & Gaddam, S. (2012). *A Billion Wicked Thoughts*. Plume.

Nimbi, F.M., Tripodi, F., Rossi, R., Navarro-Cremades,F., Simonelli, Chiara (2019). Male Sexual Desire: An Overview of Biological, Psychological, Sexual, Relational, and Cultural Factors Influencing Desire. DOI:https://doi.org/10.1016/j.sxmr.2018.12.002

Perel, E. (2007). *Mating in Captivity*. Harper Collins.

Preston, S. D., & De Waal, F. B. M. (2002). Empathy: Its ultimate and proximate bases. *Behavioral and brain sciences*, 25(1), 1-20.

Remes, O., Brayne, C., van der Linde. R., & Lafortune, L. (2016). A systematic review of reviews on the prevalence of anxiety disorders in adult populations. Brain and Behavior, https://doi.org/10.1002/brb3.497

Rosenberg, S. (1984). Changing the Vision: Prescription for Peace. *Voices: the Art and Science of Psychotherapy*, 20), 46-47.

Rosin, H. (2010). The End of Men: How Women are Taking Control of Everything. Retrieved December 31, 2018.

Siegel, D. (2010). *Mindsight: The New Science of Personal Transformation*. New York: W.W. Norton.

Vandello, J. A., & Bosson, J. K. (2013). Hard won and easily lost: A review and synthesis of theory and research on precarious manhood. *Psychology of Men & Masculinity*, 14(2), 101.

Weiss, A. G. (2002). The lost role of dependency in psychotherapy. *Gestalt Review*, 6(1), 6-17.

About the Author

Avrum G. Weis, Ph.D. is a clinical psychologist who sees individuals and couples for psychotherapy online. Dr. Weiss is recognized nationally for his pioneering work on the process of change in individuals and organizations.

Published Books

- *Change Happens: When to Try Harder and When to Stop Trying So Hard*, Rowman & Littlefield Publishers (November 3, 2011) http://bit.ly/AvrumWeissChangeHappens

- *Living and Loving Mutually: How To Break Free From Hurtful Relationship Patterns*, Lasting Impact Press, an imprint of Connection Victory Publishing Company (November 2020) https://www.amazon.com/Living-Loving-Mutually-Relationship-Patterns/dp/1643810316/

- *Hidden in Plain Sight: How Men's Fears of Women Shape Their Intimate Relationships,* Lasting Impact Press, an imprint of Connection Victory Publishing Company (September 2021) https://www.amazon.com/Hidden-Plain-Sight-Intimate-Relationships-ebook/dp/B09DTNR6ZC/

Articles/Columns by Avrum G. Weiss, Ph.D.

- Psychology Today:
  https://www.psychologytoday.com/us/therapists/avrum-geurin-weiss-atlanta-ga/42420
- The Good Men Project:
  https://goodmenproject.com/author/agweiss/

Connect With the Author

- Facebook: Page
  https://www.FB.com/AvrumWeissAuthor/
- Facebook Group:
  https://bit.ly/MensFearsOfWomenAvrumWeissFBGroup
- Landing page: https://bit.ly/AvrumWeissBooks
- Twitter: https://twitter.com/avrum_weiss
- To book a guest lecture or other speaking engagement:
  inforequest@connectionvictory.com
- Dr. Avrum Weiss' email address:
  <agweiss@comcast.net>

License and Foreign Rights

For information on obtaining a license to use this content, contact the publisher: <inforequest@connectionvictory.com>.

Also Published by Lasting Impact Press an Imprint of Connection Victory Publishing Company

Listed in order of first publication date.

1. *How to Cope, Manage the Household, and Make Love When Your Wife Has Cancer: Practical Guidance for the Husband-Caregiver* by Michael D. Stalter, January 2016

2. *Curbing Human Trafficking: Sex slavery is a horrific international crime against women, men, and children. You can help stop it.* by Mark J. Vruno, December 2017

3. *A Broken System: Family Court in The United States, Volume 1* by Stephen Louis Krasner, February 2018

4. *Man Box: Poems* by Cameron Conaway, April 2018

5. *Love 5.0: The Secrets for Being Close Yet Free and Having a Marriage That Lasts Forever* by Jed Diamond, Ph.D., April 2018

6. *How Did You Get Him To Eat That? 12 Parenting Practices That Lead to Healthy Eating* by John D Rich, Ph.D., June 2018

7. *My Distant Dad: Healing the Family Father Wound* by Jed Diamond, Ph.D., June 2018

8. *Healing the Family Father Wound: Your Playbook for Personal and Relationship Success*, by Jed Diamond, Ph.D. August 2018

9. *A Broken System: Family Court in The United States, Volume 2* by Stephen Louis Krasner, September 2018

10. *Positive Parenting: A Practical and Sometimes Humorous Approach To Applying The Research In Your Home With Gender Inclusivity, Mutual Respect, and Empathy – and NO Spanking!* By John D Rich, Ph.D., February 2019

11. *Practical Parenting: A Workbook To Accompany Positive Parenting* by John D Rich, Ph.D.

12. *tumbling: poetic thoughts from an anxious mind by Elizabeth Joyce*, November 2019

13. *The Resilient WriterWheels: Can't Is A Bad Word* by Erin M. Kelly, May 2020

14. *Living and Loving Mutually:How To Break Free From Hurtful Relationship Patterns* by Avrum G. Weiss, Ph.D. November 2020

15. *Talkin' to You, Bro: Liberating Yourself From the Confusing and Ambiguous Messages of Contemporary Masculinity* by Elwood David Watson, Ph.D.,, September 21, 2021

16. Hidden in Plain Sight: How Men's Fears of Women Shape Their Intimate Relationships by Avrum G. Weiss, Ph.D., September 2021

Coming Soon from Lasting Impact Press, an Imprint of Connection Victory Publishing Company

Mick & Me: My Unlikely Friendship With Wrestling Legend Mick Foley by Erin M. Kelly, Fall 2021

www.ingramcontent.com/pod-product-compliance
Lightning Source LLC
Chambersburg PA
CBHW060509280326
41933CB00014B/2901